Where Is It From?

by Ellen Dalton

smereka/Shutterstock.com

What is bread made from?

What is rope made from?

What is popcorn made from?

What is paper made from?

What is glass made from?

What is chocolate made from?

What is this made from?

Yum!

Where Is It From?

Talk to your partner about the book. Where is bread from? Where is popcorn from?

I Use This

Draw a picture of something you use every day. Write a sentence for your picture.

I use ________.

Nature

Pre K • Unit 8 Week 1

mhreadingwonders.com

978-0-07-678420-2
MHID 0-07-678420-7

EAN
9 780076 784202
99701

McGraw Hill Education

Fantasía

¡Sí y no!

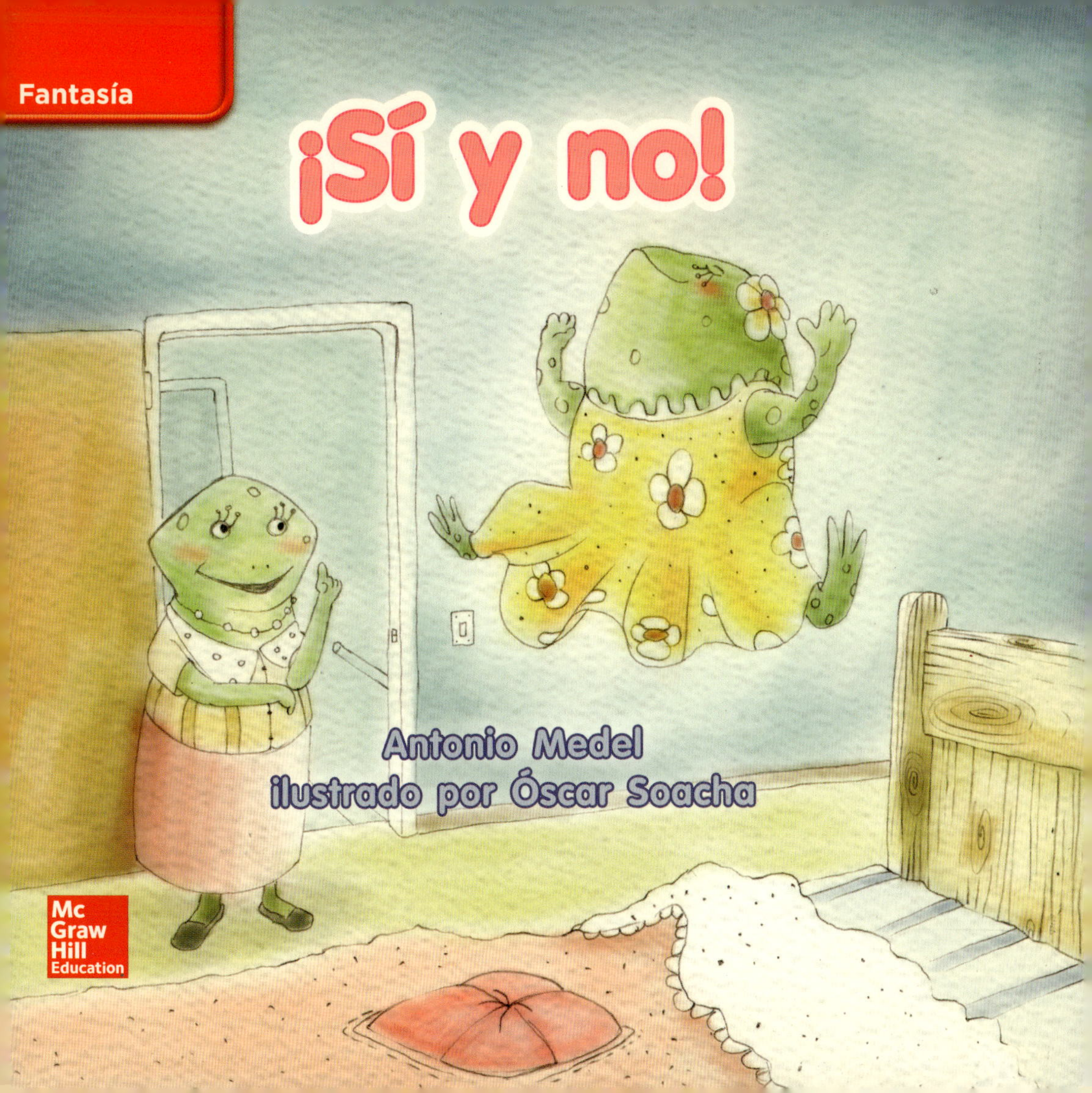

Antonio Medel
ilustrado por Óscar Soacha

McGraw Hill Education

ESTRATEGIAS Y DESTREZAS

Comprensión

Estrategia: Visualizar

Destreza: Detalles clave

Palabra de uso frecuente

ella

Fonética

Sonido /n/

Número de palabras: 22

mheducation.com/prek-12

Send all inquiries to:
McGraw-Hill Education
Two Penn Plaza
New York, New York 10121

ISBN: 978-0-02-125959-5
MHID: 0-02-125959-3

Printed in China.

6 7 8 9 10 DSS 22 21 20 19 18 B